Abstinence

Postponing Sexual Involvement

By Judith Peacock

Consultant:
Jennifer A. Oliphant, MPH
Research Fellow and Community Outreach Coordinator
National Teen Pregnancy Prevention Research Center
Division of General Pediatrics and Adolescent Health
University of Minnesota

Perspectives on Healthy Sexuality

LifeMatters
an imprint of Capstone Press
Mankato, Minnesota

LifeMatters Books are published by Capstone Press
PO Box 669 • 151 Good Counsel Drive • Mankato, Minnesota 56002
http://www.capstone-press.com

Printed in the United States of America

Library of Congress Cataloging-in-Publication Data
Peacock, Judith, 1942–
      Abstinence: postponing sexual involvement / by Judith Peacock.
           p.   cm.—(Perspectives on healthy sexuality)
      Includes bibliographical references and index.
      ISBN 0-7368-0713-6 (hard cover) ISBN 0-7368-8842-X (soft cover)
      1. Sexual abstinence—Juvenile literature. [1. Sexual abstinence.] I. Title. II. Series.
      HQ800.15 .P4 2001
      306.73´2—dc21   00-039107
                                                      CIP

Summary: Explains abstinence and its benefits; discusses the challenges of being abstinent as well as ways to maintain abstinence and deal with sexual pressure.

Staff Credits
Rebecca Aldridge, editor; Adam Lazar, designer; Kim Danger, photo researcher
Production by Stacey Field

Photo Credits
Cover: ©PhotoDisc/Barbara Penoyar
©Artville/Don Castons, 11, 27, 28, 42
Photo Network/©Bachmann, 8; ©Esbin-Anderson, 15, 33, 59; ©Myrleen Cate, 34
©StockByte, 7
Unicorn Stock Photos/©Tom McCarthy, 23; ©Creative Photographic Images, 55; ©Karen Holsinger Mullen, 56
Uniphoto/18, ©Michael A. Keller, 17; ©Jeffry W. Myers, 24; ©Bob Daemmrich, 37; ©Llewellyn, 45; ©Daemmrich, 48
UPmagazine/©Tim Yoon, 39
Visuals Unlimited/©D. Yeske, 46

Table of Contents

Chapter Overview

Sexual abstinence means avoiding sexual intercourse. Teens who choose abstinence postpone having vaginal, oral, and anal intercourse.

Some teens who choose abstinence avoid kissing, making out, and other forms of sexual touching that might lead to intercourse.

The number of American teens choosing abstinence is growing.

Anyone can choose to be abstinent. Even people who have been sexually active can decide to be abstinent.

Teens need to decide for themselves whether to have sexual relations. A decision-making process can help teens choose what's right for them.

Chapter 1

What Is Abstinence?

Tyler is a popular athlete and a leader in his high school class. Tyler has never had

Tyler, Age 17

sexual intercourse. It's not that he hasn't had the opportunity or that he doesn't want to have sex. Like many teen boys, Tyler thinks about girls and sex a lot. What's more, girls like him. For now, however, Tyler has decided to postpone having sex. He has chosen sexual abstinence.

The word *abstinence* comes from *abstain*, which means to stay away from or to avoid something. People may choose to abstain from many things. People who abstain from meat don't eat meat. People who abstain from alcohol don't drink beer, whiskey, wine, or any other alcoholic drinks. People who abstain from sex don't have sexual relations.

Single and married adults may practice abstinence for different reasons and for different lengths of time. They may be abstinent because of illness or injury or because their partner is absent. They may not be able to find a suitable partner.

Some couples abstain from sex during a woman's fertile time of the month. This is when the woman is most likely to get pregnant. Abstaining from sex during a woman's fertile time is called periodic abstinence. It's a form of birth control.

Teens and Abstinence

Teens who choose sexual abstinence still can go out on dates and have fun. They still can have a boyfriend or girlfriend. These teens simply have decided to limit their sexual activity.

Sexual Relations

Sexual abstinence often refers to avoiding vaginal intercourse. Vaginal intercourse occurs when the male's penis penetrates the female's vagina. Sexual abstinence also can include avoiding anal and oral intercourse. Anal intercourse is when the penis penetrates the partner's anus. Oral intercourse occurs when the penis penetrates the partner's mouth.

Some teens avoid kissing and touching in a sexual way while abstinent. These teens avoid any physical touching that could lead to intercourse. For other abstinent teens, such activities are all right—so long as they don't lead to intercourse. Teens who choose abstinence need to be clear on what abstinence means to them.

"I've chosen to be sexually abstinent. My parents helped me decide on standards, or rules, to guide me. I wrote down the standards, so I won't forget them. They include the following:

Rosa, Age 15

1. I will keep my clothes on when I am on a date.

2. Any part of my body covered by underwear is a no-go zone for my date.

3. No French-kissing.

4. If my boyfriend's hands or my hands start roaming, we'll know we've gone too far.

5. I will avoid being alone with my boyfriend in places where we might go further than we want.

6. I will be home from my date by curfew."

Postponing Sexual Relations

If a teen chooses abstinence, does that mean he or she will never have sex? Not at all. For a teen, sexual abstinence means postponing sexual relations.

The next question is, for how long? The answer often depends on the teen's reason for choosing abstinence. For example, some teens believe that sex before marriage is wrong. They may choose to remain abstinent until they marry. Other teens feel they are too young to handle a sexual relationship. They may decide to wait until they are older and emotionally ready before having sex. Some teens choose sexual abstinence until they feel they can handle the responsibilities of a long-term, committed relationship. Some wait until they feel ready for the responsibilities of birth control and protection against sexually transmitted diseases (STDs). These diseases that are spread by sexual contact also are called sexually transmitted infections (STIs).

"There are several reasons why I don't have sex. First, who would I do it with? There's no one I even like that well, much less love. Second, I can't see myself getting naked with someone. Getting dressed in the locker room after gym class is embarrassing enough. Third, I can't see myself going into a store and buying condoms or just whipping out a condom before doing it. Fourth, what if the guy dumped me? I don't think I could deal with that. I guess I'm just not ready for sex."—Dean, age 16

Who Chooses Abstinence?

You may think that only teens who can't get dates choose abstinence. This is not the case at all. Lots of teens decide that abstinence is the best choice for them. More and more teens are choosing abstinence. During the 1990s, the number of teen pregnancies in the United States plunged. Experts say that increased teen abstinence is one reason for the decline. Abstinence is not only for straight teens. Gay and lesbian teens can choose abstinence as well.

People Who Were Sexually Active

Virgins are people who have never had sexual intercourse. Abstinence may be easier for virgins than for people who have had sex. Virgins may not miss something they have never experienced. Abstinence, however, is not just for virgins. Sexually active teens can choose abstinence, too. It's never too late to choose abstinence.

Abstinence does have possible problems. People may find it hard to stay abstinent for long periods of time. Often, people stop being abstinent without being ready to protect themselves and their partner from possible pregnancy or STDs.

Double Standard

Abstinence is for males as well as for females. Unfortunately, some people think being abstinent is more important for girls than for boys. According to this view, females should remain virgins until they marry. Yet it is acceptable for males to experiment with sex. This belief is known as the double standard. It means there is one set of rules for girls and a different set of rules for boys. However, both males and females can benefit from being abstinent.

It's Your Choice

Whether to have sexual relations is an important personal decision. It can be a difficult decision for many teens. Whenever facing a hard choice, you can apply this decision-making process:

Step 1. Consider your options.

Step 2. List the benefits and possible consequences of each option.

Step 3. Think about your values, or what's important to you.

Step 4. Make your decision.

Step 5. Think carefully about whether your decision is right for you.

As you think about abstinence, remember that you are an important person. You have the right to make decisions about your own body. No one should force you into doing something that feels uncomfortable or that you are not ready to do.

Points to Consider

What is your definition of sexual abstinence? If you were to choose abstinence, what limits would you place on your sexual activity?

Do you know anyone who has declared abstinence? Describe this person's approach to abstinence.

Do you think some people believe abstinence is more important for females than for males? Why?

What does your school teach about abstinence?

Chapter Overview

Teens who choose abstinence help to protect their health and safety. Abstinence offers 100 percent protection against pregnancy and STDs if practiced perfectly and all the time.

Most teens may not be prepared to deal with the emotional effects of sexual intercourse. Teens who wait to have sex have more time to develop emotionally, intellectually, and socially. They have freedom to work toward their goals.

Teens who practice abstinence may honor their family or religious beliefs and values.

Abstinence can help teens develop long-lasting, satisfying relationships.

Abstinence can provide teens with more time to work toward personal goals.

Chapter 2

Benefits of Abstinence

Teens may choose abstinence for many different reasons. In each case, abstinence provides benefits. Saying no to sex allows teens to focus on their future without worry of STDs or pregnancy.

Avoiding Unplanned Pregnancy

Abstinence is 100 percent effective in preventing pregnancy. However, pregnancy is possible without sexual intercourse. This can happen if semen, or fluid released from the penis, gets near the vagina. Semen contains sperm, which are male sex cells.

To prevent STDs, teens who are sexually active must use male or female condoms or dental dams. Male condoms are 98 percent effective in preventing most STDs, but only if used correctly and with every act of sexual intercourse. Condoms do not protect against every STD because they do not cover every area that might become infected. Dental dams protect against STDs during oral-vaginal or oral-anal sex. Female condoms can be used as protection during anal, as well as oral, sex.

Having sex can throw teens into a world of adult responsibilities. If a girl becomes pregnant, she and her partner face hard decisions. If they decide to raise the baby, they may have to make sacrifices. Sometimes, the girl is left to raise the child alone or with her parents. Teen mothers may have difficulty finishing high school and earning a living. They and their children may live in poverty.

Avoiding STDs

Abstinence protects teens from STDs. It can be 100 percent effective provided teens strictly limit their sexual activity. Teens must be sure no body fluids such as semen, vaginal fluids, or blood are exchanged with a partner. Some STDs such as herpes and pubic lice can be transmitted through touching and kissing as well as sexual intercourse.

Having an STD can affect a teen's life, both now and in the future. Some STDs can cause infertility, or the inability to have a baby. STDs such as HIV/AIDS can cause serious illness and even death. Teens with an STD may need to take medications for the rest of their life. People with an STD must use protection such as condoms or abstain from sexual activity to prevent spreading the disease to others.

Avoiding Emotional Consequences

Sexual intercourse involves the emotions as well as the body. Many teens say they were not prepared for how intercourse affected them emotionally. Handling the stormy feelings and changes that occur during the teen years can be difficult enough. Adding the intense emotions related to sex can overwhelm a teen. Abstinence keeps teens from having to deal with the emotional consequences of sex before they are ready.

In a national survey, teen girls gave the following reasons for abstaining from sex:

Having sex is against their moral or religious values. (44 percent)

They want to avoid getting pregnant. (20 percent)

They haven't met the appropriate partner. (20 percent)

They fear getting an STD. (13 percent)

Laura had a mental picture of what her first sexual experience would be like. She'd be with a guy she really liked and who liked her as well. They'd be in a romantic place with soft lights and music. He'd take her in his arms. . . .

Laura, Age 14

Unfortunately, Laura's first time wasn't what she had imagined. Some older kids invited Laura and her friends to a party. Laura was flattered when a senior boy began flirting with her. She quickly drank several glasses of vodka and cranberry juice. She thought being drunk would hide her nervousness. After a while, Laura and the boy went out in the backyard to talk. Before she knew it, they were on the ground under some bushes having sex.

The next day, Laura felt sick. She didn't remember many details about the sex, except that it had hurt. She couldn't recall if the boy wore a condom, but she was pretty sure he hadn't. When Laura saw the boy in the hall on Monday, he looked straight at her and then walked away.

Beliefs and Values

Some teens are taught by their family or religion that they should wait until marriage before having sexual intercourse. These teens may view sex as an expression of love and lifelong commitment to one person. Abstinence helps these teens remain true to their ideals.

Other teens believe that sexual relations should take place within a long-term, committed relationship, but not necessarily marriage. They want to have sex only with someone they love and respect and who loves and respects them in return. These teens choose abstinence while they wait for that special person.

Abstinence helps both kinds of people. Either way, with abstinence teens can remain true to their beliefs and values.

"My dad was a virgin when he married my mom at age 20. He's been happy and proud all through their life together because he held out. I want to wait, too. I've promised my parents that I'll stay abstinent until I meet the right person."

Randall, Age 15

Dating and Other Relationships

Some teens choose abstinence because it helps them develop more satisfying personal relationships without sex. On a date they can relax and have fun. They don't have to think about sex. This is because they have decided ahead of time and discussed with their parents about remaining abstinent. These teens concentrate on getting to know the other person's interests, ideas, and feelings.

Often, a teen couple who has intercourse finds that sex makes the relationship more intense. They may focus mainly on each other rather than friends. They eventually may lose some of their connection with these friends. When sex becomes part of a relationship, couples may find it more difficult to break up. Even if they are unhappy, they may stay together because of the sex.

"I've had two boyfriends. I had sex during my relationships with both of them. After my last boyfriend, Ted, broke up with me, I decided to become abstinent. That way I figure I can better get to know the next guy I date."—Angela, age 17

Time for Personal Growth

Some teens choose abstinence to allow more time for personal growth. They may want to make new friends, join clubs and teams, play sports, have jobs, or develop interests and skills. They may want time to plan for their future. These teens believe that sexual activity may distract them from reaching their goals. They also may realize that an unplanned pregnancy or STD could result in hard choices and decisions.

Points to Consider

What are some other reasons teens might choose abstinence?

What might be your reason or reasons for choosing abstinence? Why?

How could abstinence benefit a teen's reputation?

How might gay and lesbian teens benefit from abstinence?

Chapter Overview

Teens experience a surge of sexual energy that can make abstinence difficult.

Abstinence is not easy for a teen. Sometimes the pressure to have sex is difficult to overcome. Television shows, movies, and other media give the idea that casual, unprotected sex is common and has no consequences.

Peer pressure can be a challenge to staying abstinent.

Teens may receive confusing messages from adults about abstinence.

It can be tempting to break a commitment to abstinence to show love for another person.

Chapter 3

Challenges to Abstinence

Teens who choose abstinence face many challenges. This chapter describes some of these challenges. Chapters 4, 5, and 6 suggest ways to deal with them.

Teen Hormones

During puberty, the body begins producing sex hormones. These chemicals cause the sex organs to grow. The body becomes ready for sexual intercourse. Hormones also cause strong sexual urges. Teens may find themselves thinking about sex more than ever. Abstinence can be difficult when the body is full of sexual energy.

Teens are becoming physically ready for sex at a younger age than ever before. For example, the average age of a girl's first menstruation, or period, is now 12.5 years. At the same time, the average age for first marriage is rising. Half of all American women are still single at age 24. The average age at which men get married is 26. It may be hard for young people to remain sexually abstinent for the decade between physical maturity and marriage.

Meeting the Challenge

A teen's body may be ready for sex, but most likely his or her mind and emotions are not. Emotional and mental growth typically lag behind physical growth during the teen years. Be patient with yourself. Your emotions need time to catch up with your physical maturity. Sexual feelings at this age are normal. You can learn to deal with them in a healthy way.

Media Influences

The media also make choosing abstinence difficult. TV programs, movies, and advertisements constantly hit teens with images of sexual activity. They show people having sex without making a decision or discussing birth control, unplanned pregnancy, or STDs. Often, even if the characters aren't having sex, they're talking about it. Teens easily may get the message that everyone is having sex and that casual sex is common. Teens may believe that they won't seem mature unless they have sex.

Meeting the Challenge

It's important to realize that the media focus on sex because it gets people's attention. Sex helps to sell products and increase ratings. The way sex is shown in the media tends to be unrealistic and irresponsible. The media seldom have characters facing unplanned pregnancies, STDs, or other risks of sexual intercourse.

Peer Pressure

Peer pressure occurs when friends or people your own age directly or indirectly influence your behavior. Peer pressure can be powerful because teens have a strong need to belong and to be accepted by others in their age group. Teens know that those who don't follow the group may be rejected.

Many teens try to convince friends or a boyfriend or girlfriend that they must have sex. They may use arguments such as "Everyone is doing it" or "You want to be a real man (or woman), don't you?" Teens may use peer pressure to excuse their own behavior, to get something they want, or to feel in control. Peer pressure can be really hard on a teen who wants to be abstinent.

At the beginning of ninth grade, Annie and her four closest friends were all virgins. Most of them had made out with boys, and a couple of them had let boys touch their breasts.

Annie, Age 15

As the year went by, things began to change. One by one, each girl lost her virginity—except for Annie. Not that Annie wasn't interested in sex. She thought about it a lot. But Annie wanted to wait for sex until she found the right guy.

Annie listened to her friends talk on and on about having sex. They seemed to be part of a secret club to which she didn't belong. Annie wondered if she had made the right decision.

Meeting the Challenge

Remember that having sex is a choice. You decide for yourself if sexual intercourse is right for you. A person shouldn't have sexual intercourse to please or impress other people. Follow your own feelings and comfort level.

"The pressure to have sex at my school is incredible. I finally decided to sleep with a guy just to get it over with and get other kids off my back."—Pia, age 15

Remember, too, that not everyone is doing it. More than half of American teens are virgins until they are at least 17. In addition, many teens who have had sex have done so only two or three times. According to surveys, many teens who tried sex wish they hadn't or wish they had waited until they were older. Finally, some teens simply are lying when they say they've had sex.

Sex, sex, sex! That's all Kirby's friends talk about. They discuss how many girls **Kirby, Age 16** they've slept with, what it was like, where they did it. Kirby has never had sex, and he doesn't want to at this point in his life. But he pretends to be sexually active, so his friends will accept him. Kirby brags right along with the rest of the guys. He doesn't know that most of his buddies are lying, too.

Peer pressure can put you in a no-win situation. On the one hand, you may be called old-fashioned or a prude if you choose not to have sex. On the other hand, if you do have sex, you may be called easy or a slut. Although difficult, it's best to stick to what you believe and not allow others to pressure you.

In some cultures, chaperons, or adult supervisors, accompany teens on dates. Other cultures do not allow teens to date at all. By contrast, teens in the United States and Canada have much more freedom, which can make abstaining from sex difficult.

Mixed Messages

Messages about abstinence from parents or other adults may confuse teens. For example, one teen's parents might say, "We don't want you to have sex until you're married, or at least until you're older. But if you do have sex, please use protection." This message may seem to send two opposite meanings. The teen may think this means, "We're not sure you can always maintain control of yourself sexually. You might as well give up and use birth control." However, the parents probably are trying to say that they know such things as hormones and peer pressure exist. They know abstinence can be difficult. They want the teen to be protected, just in case.

Meeting the Challenge

Mixed messages can be confusing for teens. Teens who choose abstinence may need the support of parents and other adults. These teens may want adults to hold up high standards. It may be important to teens that adults believe that teens can achieve these standards. Teens confused by mixed messages may need to talk with the adult to understand the adult's reasoning. They may need to be assured that the adult believes that teens can be abstinent.

Someone You Really Like

Abstinence can be difficult when you're in the arms of someone you care about a lot. Giving up your beliefs to make the other person happy may seem like the right thing to do. However, it's not.

Mala and her boyfriend, Ron, have talked about getting married in a few  **Mala, Age 18** years. Ron is beginning to pressure Mala to have sex. He says if Mala loves him, she'll sleep with him. He can't wait until they're married to make love.

Mala loves Ron and wants to make him happy, but she also wants to be a virgin when she marries. She wonders how she'll feel if she gives in to Ron and later on they break up. Will she regret having had sex with him? Will she regret not waiting for the man she marries?

Meeting the Challenge

People should not have to sacrifice what they feel is right. What you want is as important as what your partner wants. A healthy relationship is based on respect. You never should have to prove love for someone by having sex. The right partner will respect your decision to be abstinent. Abstinence is not easy. It can be hard on a relationship.

Myth: Having sex can help you hang on to a boyfriend or girlfriend.

Fact: Sex may strengthen a relationship temporarily. However, unless a couple develops common interests and communicates with each other, the relationship may soon fall apart.

Points to Consider

What are the drawbacks or disadvantages of abstinence for teens?

Do you think that peer pressure to have sex is the same for both boys and girls? Explain.

Do you believe that teens are capable of abstinence? Explain.

Assume you've chosen to be abstinent. A friend says to you, "Couples should have sex before marriage. That way they can see if they're going to be able to get along sexually." How would you respond to your friend?

Chapter Overview

Teens who choose abstinence should let family members, friends, and dates know about their decision.

Planning a date and then sticking to the plan can help teens remain abstinent. Teens should be careful about the people they go out with and the places they go.

Abstinence programs are available to support teens who want to postpone sexual intercourse.

Teens who participate in activities are less likely to be sidetracked by a sexual relationship.

Knowing the risks of sexual intercourse can help keep teens from acting in unhealthy ways. Masturbation is a safe and healthy alternative to intercourse.

Chapter 4

How to Be Abstinent

Let's say you decide to be abstinent. Sticking with your decision can be tough. As you read in the last chapter, there are many challenges to abstinence. This chapter provides ideas to help you remain true to your values.

Believe in Your Decision

Be proud of your decision. You've thought about it long and hard and believe abstinence is right for you. Feeling confident about your choice can help you fight the pressure to have sex.

Tell Family and Friends About Your Decision

Let family and friends know about your decision to be abstinent. Saying out loud what you intend to do strengthens your position. You may then feel a responsibility to keep your word. You may want to take a vow in front of others, sign a pledge card, or write a contract.

"My advice on how to be abstinent is to keep busy. There are lots of fun things to do besides having sex."
—Roger, age 16

Wear a Physical Reminder

Some teens who choose abstinence wear something specific to remind them of their decision. The item might be a piece of clothing or jewelry.

Paul wears a silver-colored band on his ring finger. He calls it his "promise ring." He never takes it off. When Paul feels tempted to be sexual with someone, he looks at the ring. It reminds him of his promise to abstain from sex. Sometimes Paul uses the ring to explain his decision to friends and classmates. Someday Paul will give the ring to the woman he marries.

Paul, Age 16

Be Up Front With Your Date or Boyfriend or Girlfriend

Talk with your date or boyfriend or girlfriend about your decision to be abstinent before things get physical. Make your limits clear before he or she gets sexually excited. Let your date know how much you enjoy being with him or her.

Your decision may come as a relief to your date. He or she may not want to have sexual relations either. Your decision may earn you respect.

It's also important to be up front with friends and classmates. Make your position on abstinence known early in conversations about sex. When peers know where you stand, they may be more likely to support you.

Mary Kay got a summer job at a camp in another state. She would be gone for two months. Mary Kay's girlfriends told her she had to have sex with her boyfriend, Jim, before she left. They said having sex would tie Jim to Mary Kay and make him faithful to her over the summer. Mary Kay is a virgin. She asked her friends to back off. "I don't believe in using sex to control other people," she told them. "Besides, maybe being apart will be a good test of our feelings for each other. If Jim and I still want to date after I get back, maybe we're really in love!"

Mary Kay, Age 17

Date Teens Your Own Age
If you date someone older than yourself, you may have difficulty resisting sexual pressure. Older teens can lead younger teens into situations and relationships that may harm the younger teen.

Avoid Going Out With Only One Person

Dating only one person increases the chances of sexual relations. If you are seeing one person, limit the amount of time you spend with him or her. Leave time for other friends and activities. A relationship should be based on friendship and common interests. If a couple spends all their time making out, they don't have time for friends, fun, or other things.

Plan Your Dates

Decide in advance what you will do on a date. Let your date know what time you need to be home. When the planned part is over, the date is over. Having free time and leaving things to chance can make it easy to lose control of the situation.

Go Out With a Group of Friends or Double Date

Going out with a group of friends makes it less likely that you'll have sexual contact with your date. Group dating takes pressure off in other ways, too. You don't have to worry about keeping up a conversation with your date. Someone else in the group usually will have something to say.

Fast Fact

Among teen mothers ages 15 to 17, about one in four has a partner who is at least five years older. Many of these girls report that they didn't really want to have sex in the first place.

Avoid Risky Situations and Activities

Avoid parties where alcohol and other drugs are being used. Alcohol and other drugs interfere with determination and the ability to make decisions. Also avoid being home alone with your date or boyfriend or girlfriend. Having sex may be tempting in this situation.

Plan where you are going to go. Places with lots of other people around are good spots to go on a date. You might try hanging out at a bowling alley, an amusement park, or the mall. If you go to a party, check to see that adults will be around to supervise.

Sometimes teens like to experiment but without actual intercourse. Such experimenting can lead to unwanted intercourse. It can be difficult to stop once a teen and his or her partner are sexually excited.

Zach likes Brittany a lot. One day, Brittany invited Zach over to her house to study. When Zach got there, Brittany suggested they study in her bedroom. Zach, who is trying to be abstinent, didn't think this was a good idea. He pictured Brittany and himself messing around on Brittany's bed. Zach didn't want that to happen. He said they should study at the kitchen table or go to the library. Brittany agreed to study in the kitchen.

Seek the Support of Others Who Believe in Abstinence

There's strength in numbers. Make friends with teens who share your belief. You can talk about problems and concerns and encourage each other to remain abstinent. This is positive peer pressure. Give your friends permission to ask you about your physical relationship with the people you date. Your friends may be able to spot trouble coming before you do.

You may be able to participate in an abstinence group or program at your school or in your community. If no group is available, consider starting one of your own. Many teens find support for abstinence through their religious or spiritual community. Some teens may want to ask a spiritual leader for guidance. The *Useful Addresses and Internet Sites* section at the back of this book lists organizations that can help with abstinence.

Build Your Self-Esteem

Self-esteem means how you feel about yourself. You can build self-esteem by working hard in school, developing your interests and talents, and helping others. There are many school and community activities in which you can get involved.

Set Goals for Your Future

Think about where you want to be 5 or 10 years from now. Work on ways to get things you want, such as a scholarship or a training program. Focus on your future. Then you are less likely to get involved in a sexual relationship that could throw you off track.

Learn the Facts About Pregnancy and STDs

Teens who know the facts about pregnancy and STDs aren't likely to be fooled into doing something risky. These teens can help other teens by telling them the facts. Teens can use the time when they are abstinent to learn about birth control and protection. Then they will be prepared to act responsibly when they decide they're ready for a sexual relationship.

Opinions differ about birth control and protection. Some people think teens who choose abstinence should keep condoms and other contraceptives on hand. They say that even abstinent teens should be prepared in case they change their mind about having sex. Other people say that encouraging teens to have birth control available makes them believe they will fail at being abstinent.

Here are some facts teens should know about pregnancy and STDs:

A girl can get pregnant the first time she has sex.

A girl can become pregnant even during her period.

A girl can become pregnant without having intercourse. Pregnancy can occur if sperm are leaked near the vagina. Sperm even can enter the vagina through underwear.

Withdrawal is a risky form of birth control. The male may not be able to withdraw his penis from the female's vagina in time to prevent ejaculation.

Symptoms of some STDs may not appear for several days to several years. A person may be infected and not know it.

Use Self-Pleasuring to Relieve Sexual Tension

Masturbation is an option for relieving sexual tension. It means rubbing the sex organs for pleasure. Masturbation does not cause physical problems and can be a healthy alternative for sexual intercourse.

Sexual daydreaming also relieves sexual tension. You may imagine yourself having sex with a movie star or sports hero. Sexual daydreaming is natural for teens.

Use Outercourse to Relieve Sexual Tension

Teens who choose abstinence do not have sexual intercourse. They may or may not choose to have outercourse. This is a way of achieving sexual pleasure without penetration of the penis into the vagina, mouth, or anus. It includes mutual masturbation, which means rubbing a partner's sex organs or rubbing your own genitals in the presence of a partner. Outercourse easily can lead to sex if couples do not discipline themselves.

Start Over

What should you do if you don't stay abstinent? Think about what happened. Try to figure out why you weren't able to stay abstinent. Next time, you can make a different choice. You may want to reread the suggestions for abstinence in this chapter for help.

Points to Consider

How can parents help teens be abstinent?

What are some interesting, fun, and nonsexual ways for teens to spend time with a date?

Do you think teens who choose abstinence should be prepared with birth control and protection? Explain.

How could you help a friend be abstinent?

Chapter Overview

Saying no to pressure to have sex can be difficult. It can be easier if you firmly believe in your decision to be abstinent.

You can say no to sex with both words and body language. It is important to be firm, honest, and direct.

Setting limits on sexual activity ahead of time and practicing responses can help you handle sexual advances.

Consider whether you want a relationship with someone who won't take no for an answer.

Chapter 5

Saying No to Sexual Pressure

Clint invited Molly, a girl he had a crush on, to a friend's party. Toward the end of the evening, someone turned the lights down low. Couples began making out. Clint and Molly found a dark corner and started kissing. Before Clint knew what was happening, Molly's hand was on his penis. She started saying something about getting it on. "What am I going to do?" thought Clint. "I'm not ready for sex!"

Clint, Age 16

Teens who try to be abstinent still may find themselves in sexual situations that seem hard to handle. Saying no to sexual pressure can be difficult. You may not want to hurt the other person's feelings. You may worry that the other person will reject you. This chapter contains tips for how to say no effectively.

Saying No Starts With You

Saying no starts with you. A teen must believe firmly in abstinence. Teens who choose abstinence must limit their sexual activity. These teens should talk with dates about staying abstinent before they are in a sexual situation. They also must decide ahead of time how to handle a sexual situation.

Two Ways to Say No

There are two ways to say no. One way is verbally, or with words. The other way is with body language. Body language includes facial expressions, gestures, posture, body closeness, touch, and movement.

A person should use both words and body language to say no to sexual pressure. The words should match the body language. Otherwise, a date may get the wrong message or a confusing one. For example, you might say no but move closer to your date. He or she may not take your words seriously. Your date may continue his or her sexual advances. However, once you say no, no matter how you say it, the other person is responsible to stop.

Saying No Verbally

A simple "No" or "I don't want to" should be enough to stop a date's sexual advance. You don't need to apologize or make excuses. Excuses can give the impression that you are not in control. Your date might be able to talk you out of excuses such as "I've had a bad day" or "We might get caught." If you want to give a reason, be honest and direct. You might say something like the following:

> "I'm planning to go to college. I don't want pregnancy or a disease to get in the way."

> "I'm playing sports. I can't risk getting sick."

> "I believe that sex outside marriage is wrong. I'm waiting for the person I marry."

> "I took a vow to be abstinent until I turn 20. My parents, my friends, and I would be disappointed if I broke my promise."

> "I care about you, but I don't want the responsibilities that go with having sex."

"My parents told me to blame them whenever someone starts putting the move on me. I say, 'My parents wouldn't like it if I had sex.'"—Libby, age 15

Be sure to say "No" and not "I don't think so." Saying "I don't think so" lacks strength. Your date might think you could be persuaded with just a little more pressure. Remember, too, that you have a right to assert yourself. After all, it's your body.

Show confidence in your decision to be abstinent. Speak calmly and firmly. A teasing, or playful, tone of voice shouldn't be used. It could be heard wrongly as an invitation for sex.

Show respect for your date. Let the person know that you enjoy his or her company but that you are not ready for sex. Be clear that it is the sex you are rejecting and not the person. You can say no and still be kind.

Saying No With Body Language

When you say no, use eye contact. Look the person in the eye. Make your facial expression neutral or serious. Stop any physical show of affection. Move away from the person. Sit up or stand up to emphasize your point. If necessary, leave the room.

Avoid body language that signals doubt or lack of confidence. For example, don't put your hand over your mouth or stare at the floor.

Brandon and Darshelle **Brandon and Darshelle, Age 17** are sitting next to each other while watching TV. Brandon's left hand traces small circles on Darshelle's palm, which is resting on her lap. His hand strays to Darshelle's waist. He starts playing with the zipper on her jeans.

"Uh oh," thinks Darshelle.

"We've been going out for about six months now, haven't we? We love each other, right?" Brandon asks softly.

Darshelle nods.

"Don't you think it's about time we took the next step?"

"You mean sex? You know I've told you that I'm not ready for sex," Darshelle replies calmly. She quietly and firmly removes his hand from her jeans.

"But you said you loved me," Brandon persists.

"Yes, but you're talking about sex, not love."

Brandon and Darshelle...

"You know you really want to do it."

"If I wanted to do it, I wouldn't be arguing with you about it."

"Everybody's doing it. Come on, Darshelle."

"Well, I'm not everybody. Besides, I don't believe everybody's doing it."

Brandon gives his final argument. "But a guy has needs! Help me out here!"

Darshelle jumps up. "I need you to respect me. When I say no, I mean no. I think I'd better go home."

"Wait, Darshelle, I'm sorry. I'll stop," Brandon pleads.

Comebacks for Pressure Lines

Pressure lines are statements people make to try to get someone to have sex. Some lines have been around a long time. Some are new. Pressure lines are selfish and insincere. They are not expressions of love.

Comebacks are replies to pressure lines. You may want to learn some comebacks. They can help you talk your way out of a pressure situation. The following chart gives examples of pressure lines and comebacks.

Put-off moves are another way to say no. You can jump up and say, "I have to call home" or "I have to go to the bathroom."

Examples of Pressure Lines and Comebacks

"Everyone else is doing it."	"Then you shouldn't have any trouble finding someone else to do it with."
"If you love me, you'll have sex with me."	"If you love me, you'll respect my feelings. You won't push me into doing something I'm not ready for."
"You want it as much as I do."	"No, I really don't. I have plans for my life, and I don't want to mess them up by getting pregnant (getting you pregnant)."
"Let's do it just this once."	"It only takes once to get an STD."
"If you won't have sex with me, I'm leaving."	"If that's all you want from me, then you should leave."
"But you used to say yes."	"That's right. But I've changed. I'm saying no now."
"Making love will make our love stronger."	"Having sex doesn't make a relationship stronger. It only complicates things."

Practice, Practice, Practice

Sometimes when teens are under sexual pressure, they get nervous and can't think of what to do or say. Such teens may find themselves being swept up in the moment. They may just let things happen. Practicing responses ahead of time can help you in such situations. Rehearse in front of a mirror or in front of a group of friends.

Saying No to Peers

Friends or classmates may push you to have sex. Tell them how you feel right away or tell them to back off. Make your words and body language match. Also, your facial expression should be serious. You might say something like the following:

"I know we're friends, but my sex life is my business."

"Don't worry about what my boyfriend or girlfriend and I do. We're getting along just fine."

"Why don't you respect my privacy?"

If You're in Trouble

You may find yourself in a situation where saying no doesn't seem to work. You may sense you're in danger of being hurt. Trust your feelings and get out of the situation as quickly as possible. Don't worry about hurting your date's feelings. You may need to say loudly and clearly, "Let go of me! Stop touching me. You're going too far." Push the person away or use other physical force if necessary.

What If You're Dumped?

A big reason teens have difficulty saying no is fear of rejection. You may succeed in getting your date to stop making sexual advances. As a result, he or she may decide to stop seeing you. If this happens, consider whether you really want to be with a person who doesn't respect you. Congratulate yourself on having the courage to stick with your decision.

Points to Consider

How could you help a younger brother or sister learn to say no to sexual pressure?

How would you say no to sexual pressure from friends or other people your age?

What are some other pressure lines a boy or girl might use with a date? How would you answer each one?

Sexual intercourse is not necessary to show love for another person. There are many other ways to express love.

The most rewarding love relationships share both emotional and physical intimacy. Couples feel close in spirit and body.

Teens who choose abstinence need to develop good communication and negotiation skills. Conflict may develop when partners do not agree on abstinence.

Sexual intercourse is most meaningful and enjoyable when experienced in a close, committed relationship. Answering some questions truthfully may help a couple determine if they are really in love.

Chapter 6

Intimacy and Abstinence

You may wonder, "How can I be abstinent and still love someone?" The answer is that love and sex are not the same. Sexual intercourse can be a wonderful and pleasurable way to express love, but it's not the only way. Many teens already may be doing other things that show love for a boyfriend or girlfriend.

Intimacy

Two people who love each other want to be close to each other. This closeness is called intimacy. Two kinds of intimacy are emotional and physical intimacy.

"You can have fun, you can be cool, and you can have a girlfriend—without having sex. The best part of a relationship is the friendship."—Danny, age 18

Emotional Intimacy

Emotional intimacy means letting the other person get close to your feelings. It means revealing your deepest thoughts and fears. Here are a few ways people in love share emotional intimacy:

Make a list of things they like about each other

Write love poems to each other

Listen to each other's problems and worries

Find out about each other's childhood

Support each other during a personal or family crisis

Tell each other what happened during their day

Have secret nicknames for each other

Have a favorite song

Share their most embarrassing moments

Physical Intimacy

Physical intimacy means being close in body to the other person. People can be physically intimate without having sexual intercourse. Here are a few of the many ways to be physically intimate:

Give each other hugs

Hold hands and go for a walk

Sit together

Snuggle up together

Work side by side on a project

Exercise together

Dance together

Put an arm around his or her partner's shoulder as comfort and encouragement

Janey and Carla love each other. All the couples they know are having sex, but not Janey and Carla. They've agreed to stay abstinent. Janey and Carla find other ways to show how they feel about each other. Janey surprises Carla by putting little notes and treats in her locker. Carla cooks Janey dinner almost every Saturday. They talk with each other on the phone every night before going to bed.

One-Way Abstinence

Sometimes one person in a relationship wants to be abstinent and the other person does not. Such a couple needs communication and negotiation, or conflict-solving, skills to work things out.

Jared and Andrea care a lot about each other. Andrea **Jared and Andrea, Age 17** wants to be abstinent, but Jared does not. They have had many conversations about waiting to have sex.

Jared is starting to pressure Andrea again. She is afraid Jared eventually will wear her down. Finally, Andrea thinks of a way to solve their conflict, although it might mean losing Jared. She tells Jared to start seeing other girls. If he finds someone else he wants to have sex with, they can break up.

The plan shocks Jared. He doesn't want to have sex with anyone but Andrea. He can't even imagine dating anyone else. Jared doesn't take Andrea up on her offer. He is more attracted to her than ever. He looks at Andrea with new admiration and respect. "I'm lucky to have a girlfriend with such strong values," he says.

Andrea used compromise to solve her conflict with Jared. In a compromise, each side gives up something. Andrea offered to give up Jared to maintain her virginity. Jared could give up Andrea to have sex with someone else. Jared saw what he really wanted was Andrea.

Sometimes negotiation doesn't work. You may have to give up a relationship to be true to your ideals and yourself.

The Real Thing

Sexual intercourse is most meaningful and pleasurable within a loving, committed relationship. Read the following statements with your boyfriend or girlfriend. Or read them separately and then compare answers. If you can answer yes to all of them, your feelings about each other truly may be love.

1. Do you want what is best for each other, even if it means not having sex?...................... Yes   No

2. Do you enjoy talking with each other?.......... Yes   No

3. Do you feel free to share your true feelings with each other?................................ Yes   No

4. Do you encourage each other to have other friends and interests?........................... Yes   No

5. Do you know each other's weaknesses but accept each other anyway?..................... Yes   No

6. If either or both of you gained 20 pounds, would you still be in love?...................... Yes   No

7. Can you talk with each other about anything and not be embarrassed?....................... Yes   No

8. Do you each have separate lives while maintaining your relationship?.................. Yes   No

9. Do you have a group of friends you do things with as a couple?................................ Yes   No

10. Are you both ready to accept the responsibilities and risks of sexual intercourse?................. Yes   No

Points to Consider

What are ways couples can show love for each other without sexual intercourse?

What is another way Andrea could have solved her conflict with Jared?

There's a saying: "Absence makes the heart grow fonder." Do you think abstinence can make the heart grow fonder?

Glossary

abstinence (AB-stuh-nenss)—choosing not to have sexual relations

condom (KON-duhm)—a barrier that fits over the penis or inside the vagina or anus

contraception (kon-truh-SEP-shuhn)—a method to prevent pregnancy

genitals (JEN-uh-tulz)—sex organs

hormone (HOR-mohn)—a chemical that controls growth and development

infertile (in-FUR-tuhl)—unable to reproduce, or have a baby

intimacy (IN-tuh-muh-see)—closeness

masturbation (mass-tur-BAY-shuhn)—rubbing or touching of the sex organs for pleasure

outercourse (OU-tur-korss)—a form of sexual pleasure without penetration of the penis into the vagina, anus, or mouth

peer pressure (PIHR PRESH-ur)—influence from people your own age to act or do something a certain way

pregnancy (PREG-nuhn-see)—the joining of a male's sperm with a female's egg that forms an unborn baby

self-esteem (SELF-ess-TEEM)—a feeling of personal pride and respect for yourself

sexual intercourse (SEK-shoo-wuhl IN-tur-korss)—penetration of the penis into the vagina, anus, or mouth

sexually transmitted disease (STD) (SEK-shoo-wuhl-lee transs-MIT-tuhd duh-ZEEZ)—a disease that is spread through sexual contact between people

virgin (VUR-jin)—a person who has not had sexual intercourse

For More Information

Bull, David. *Cool and Celibate? Sex or No Sex.* Boston: Element Children's
Books, 1998.

Endersbe, Julie K. *Teen Sex: Risks and Consequences.* Mankato, MN: Capstone,
2000.

Kreiner, Anna. *In Control: Learning to Say No to Sexual Pressure.* New York:
Rosen, 1997.

Pogany, Susan Browning. *SexSmart: 501 Reasons to Hold Off on Sex.*
Minneapolis: Fairview Press, 1998.

Useful Addresses and Internet Sites

Advocates for Youth
1025 Vermont Avenue Northwest
Suite 200
Washington, DC 20005
www.advocatesforyouth.org

Alan Guttmacher Institute
1120 Connecticut Avenue Northwest
Suite 460
Washington, DC 20036
www.agi-usa.org

Girls Incorporated National Headquarters
120 Wall Street
Third Floor
New York, NY 10005
1-800-374-4475
www.girlsinc.org

National Campaign to Prevent Teen Pregnancy
1776 Massachusetts Avenue Northwest
Suite 200
Washington, DC 20036
www.teenpregnancy.org

Planned Parenthood Federation of America
810 Seventh Avenue
New York, NY 10019
1-800-669-0156
www.plannedparenthood.org

Planned Parenthood Federation of Canada
1 Nicholas Street, Suite 430
Ottawa, ON K1N 7B7
CANADA
www.ppfc.ca

Free Teens
www.freeteens.org
Offers a reality-based HIV/AIDS, STD, and pregnancy prevention program centered on abstinence

Sexual Integrity for Teens
www.agnr.umd.edu/nnfr/adolsex/fact
Provides 14 fact sheets on sexual issues for parents and teens

ZAP (Zero Adolescent Pregnancy)
www.cortlandny.com/zap
Gives information on how one community works to prevent teen pregnancy

Index